VOL. 83

HAL•LEONARD

GUITAR

PLAY-ALONG®

THREE CHORD SONGS

ISBN 978-1-4234-3084-1

HAL•LEONARD®
CORPORATION

7777 W. BLUEMOUND RD. P.O. BOX 13819 MILWAUKEE, WI 53213

For all works contained herein:
Unauthorized copying, arranging, adapting, recording, Internet posting, public performance, or other distribution
of the printed or recorded music in this publication is an infringement of copyright.
Infringers are liable under the law.

Visit Hal Leonard Online at
www.halleonard.com

Guitar Notation Legend

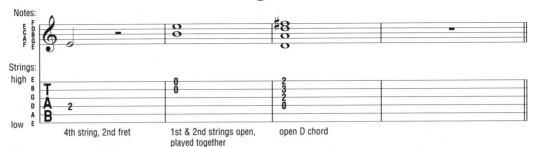

THE MUSICAL STAFF shows pitches and rhythms and is divided by bar lines into measures. Pitches are named after the first seven letters of the alphabet.

TABLATURE graphically represents the guitar fingerboard. Each horizontal line represents a string, and each number represents a fret.

4th string, 2nd fret   1st & 2nd strings open, played together   open D chord

HALF-STEP BEND: Strike the note and bend up 1/2 step.

WHOLE-STEP BEND: Strike the note and bend up one step.

GRACE NOTE BEND: Strike the note and immediately bend up as indicated.

SLIGHT (MICROTONE) BEND: Strike the note and bend up 1/4 step.

BEND AND RELEASE: Strike the note and bend up as indicated, then release back to the original note. Only the first note is struck.

PRE-BEND: Bend the note as indicated, then strike it.

VIBRATO: The string is vibrated by rapidly bending and releasing the note with the fretting hand.

PALM MUTING: The note is partially muted by the pick hand lightly touching the string(s) just before the bridge.

HAMMER-ON: Strike the first (lower) note with one finger, then sound the higher note (on the same string) with another finger by fretting it without picking.

PULL-OFF: Place both fingers on the notes to be sounded. Strike the first note and without picking, pull the finger off to sound the second (lower) note.

LEGATO SLIDE: Strike the first note and then slide the same fret-hand finger up or down to the second note. The second note is not struck.

SHIFT SLIDE: Same as legato slide, except the second note is struck.

TRILL: Very rapidly alternate between the notes indicated by continuously hammering on and pulling off.

TAPPING: Hammer ("tap") the fret indicated with the pick-hand index or middle finger and pull off to the note fretted by the fret hand.

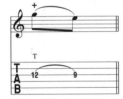

NATURAL HARMONIC: Strike the note while the fret-hand lightly touches the string directly over the fret indicated.

PINCH HARMONIC: The note is fretted normally and a harmonic is produced by adding the edge of the thumb or the tip of the index finger of the pick hand to the normal pick attack.

TREMOLO PICKING: The note is picked as rapidly and continuously as possible.

VIBRATO BAR DIVE AND RETURN: The pitch of the note or chord is dropped a specified number of steps (in rhythm), then returned to the original pitch.

VIBRATO BAR SCOOP: Depress the bar just before striking the note, then quickly release the bar.

VIBRATO BAR DIP: Strike the note and then immediately drop a specified number of steps, then release back to the original pitch.

Additional Musical Definitions

(accent) • Accentuate note (play it louder).

(staccato) • Play the note short.

D.S. al Coda • Go back to the sign (%), then play until the measure marked "*To Coda*," then skip to the section labelled "**Coda**."

D.C. al Fine • Go back to the beginning of the song and play until the measure marked "*Fine*" (end).

Fill • Label used to identify a brief melodic figure which is to be inserted into the arrangement.

N.C. • Harmony is implied.

• Repeat measures between signs.

• When a repeated section has different endings, play the first ending only the first time and the second ending only the second time.

AL·LEONARD

GUITAR
PLAY-ALONG®

VOL. 83

THREE CHORD SONGS

CONTENTS

Bye Bye Love

Words and Music by Felice Bryant and Boudleaux Bryant

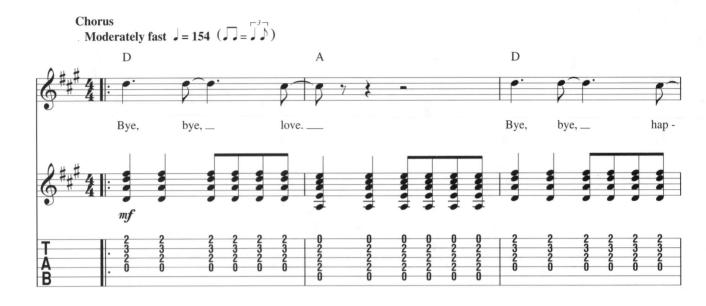

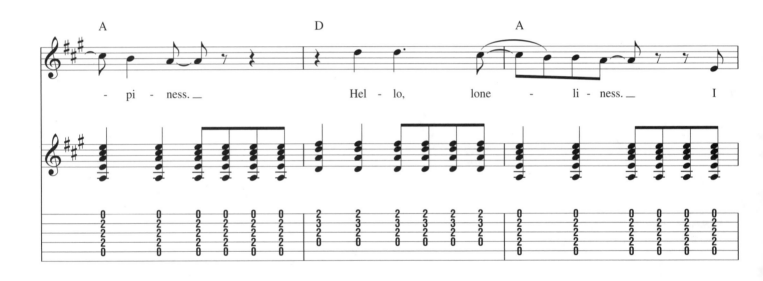

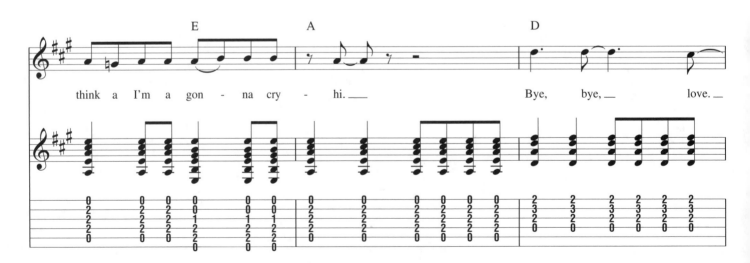

Copyright © 1957 by HOUSE OF BRYANT PUBLICATIONS, Gatlinburg, TN
Copyright Renewed
All Foreign Rights Controlled by SONY/ATV MUSIC PUBLISHING LLC
All Rights for SONY/ATV MUSIC PUBLISHING LLC Administered by SONY/ATV MUSIC PUBLISHING LLC, 8 Music Square West, Nashville, TN 37203
International Copyright Secured   All Rights Reserved

2nd time, D.C. al Coda

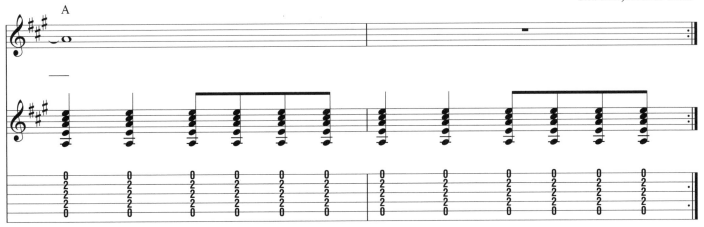

Repeat and fade

Additional Lyrics

2. I'm through with romance,
   I'm through with love.
   I'm through with countin' the stars above.
   And here's the reason that I'm so free:
   My lovin' baby is through with me.

Gloria

Words and Music by Van Morrison

Intro
Moderately fast ♩ = 130

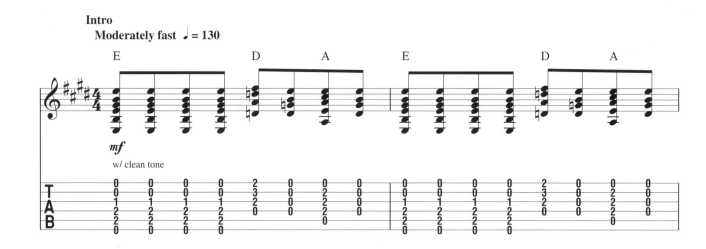

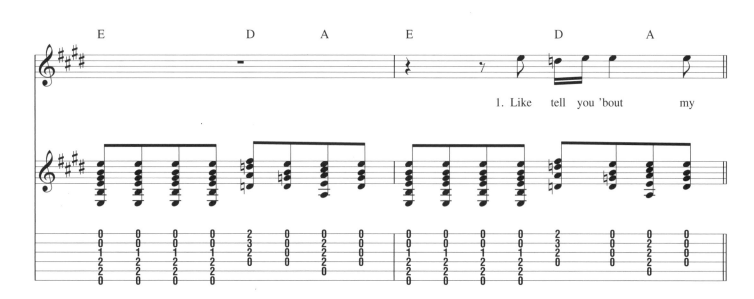

1. Like tell you 'bout my

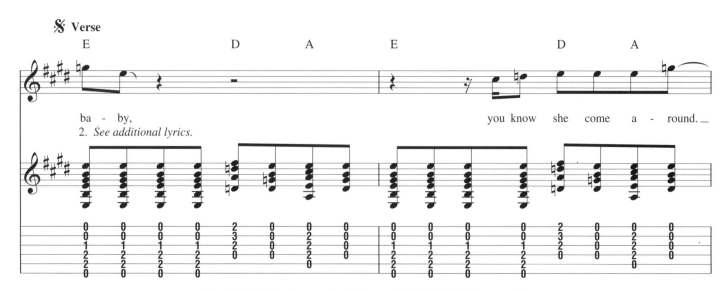

ba - by,
2. *See additional lyrics.*

you know she come a - round. _

Copyright © 1965 by January Music Corp. and Hyde Park Music Company Ltd.
Copyright Renewed
Published in the U.S.A. and Canada by Unichappell Music Inc. and Bernice Music, Inc.
All Rights Administered by Unichappell Music Inc.
International Copyright Secured   All Rights Reserved

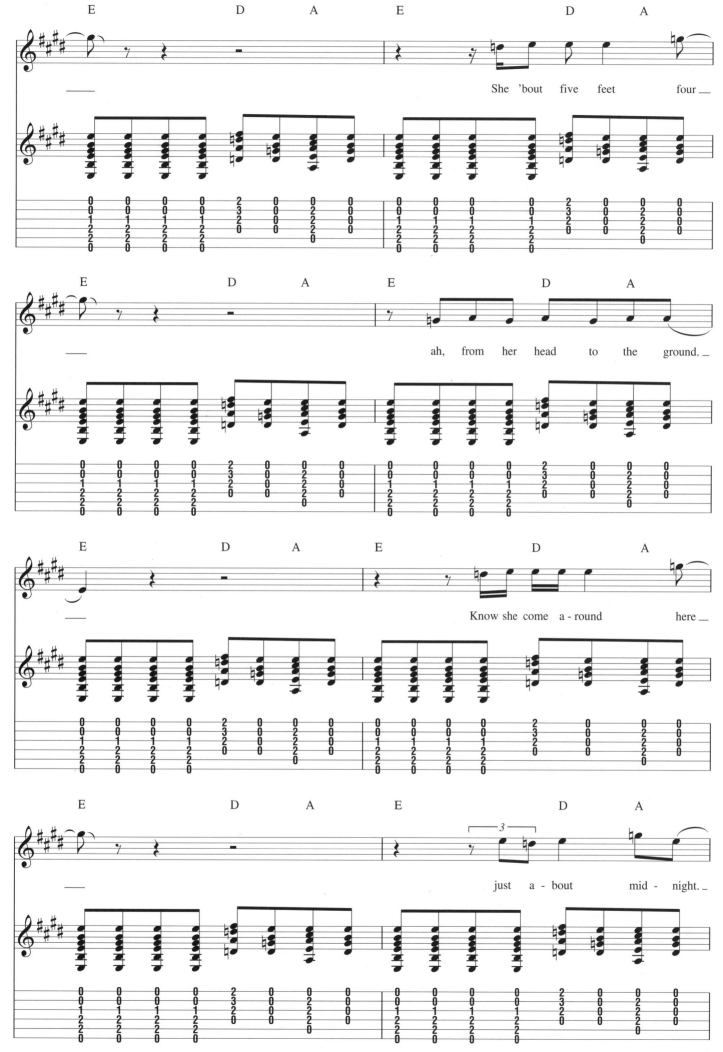

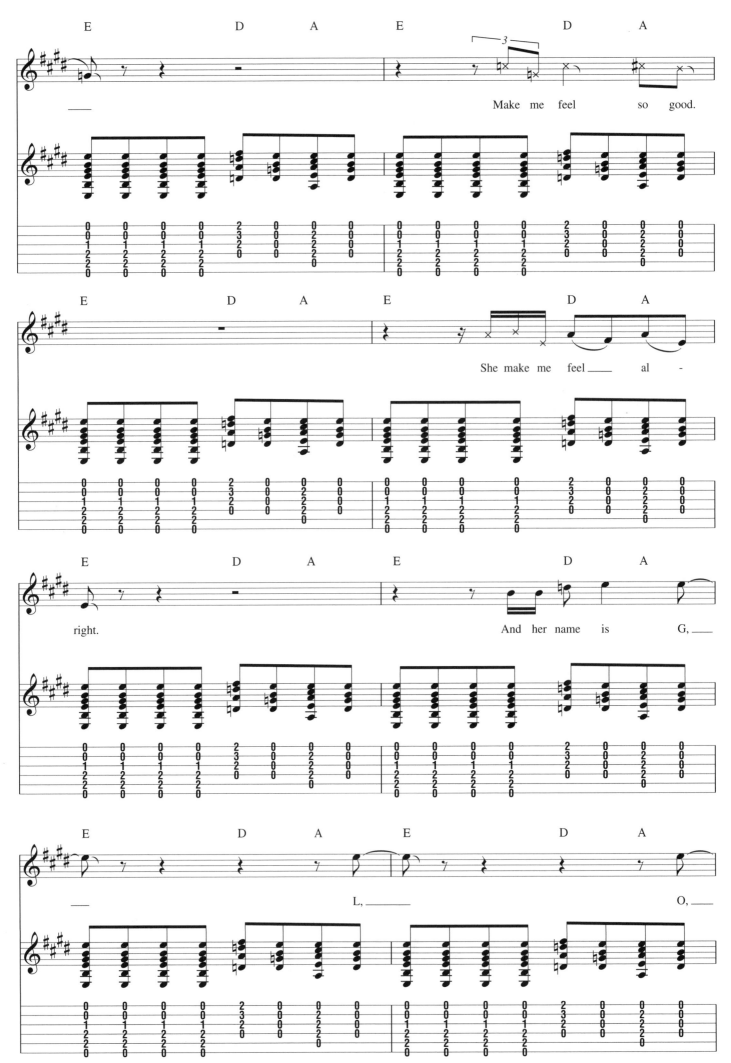

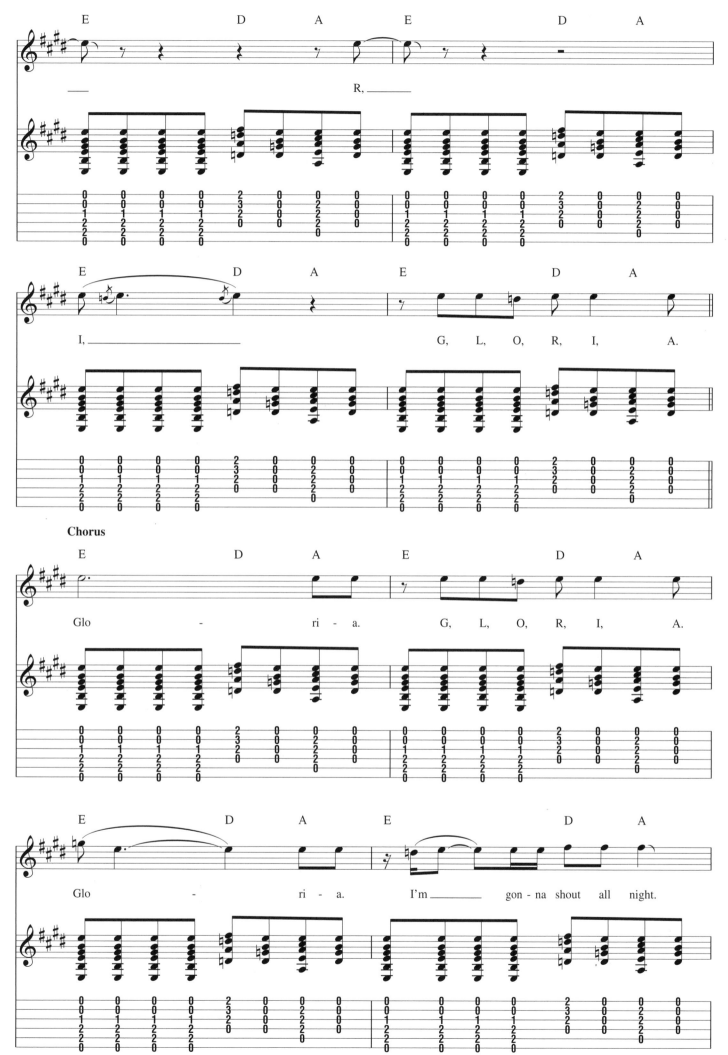

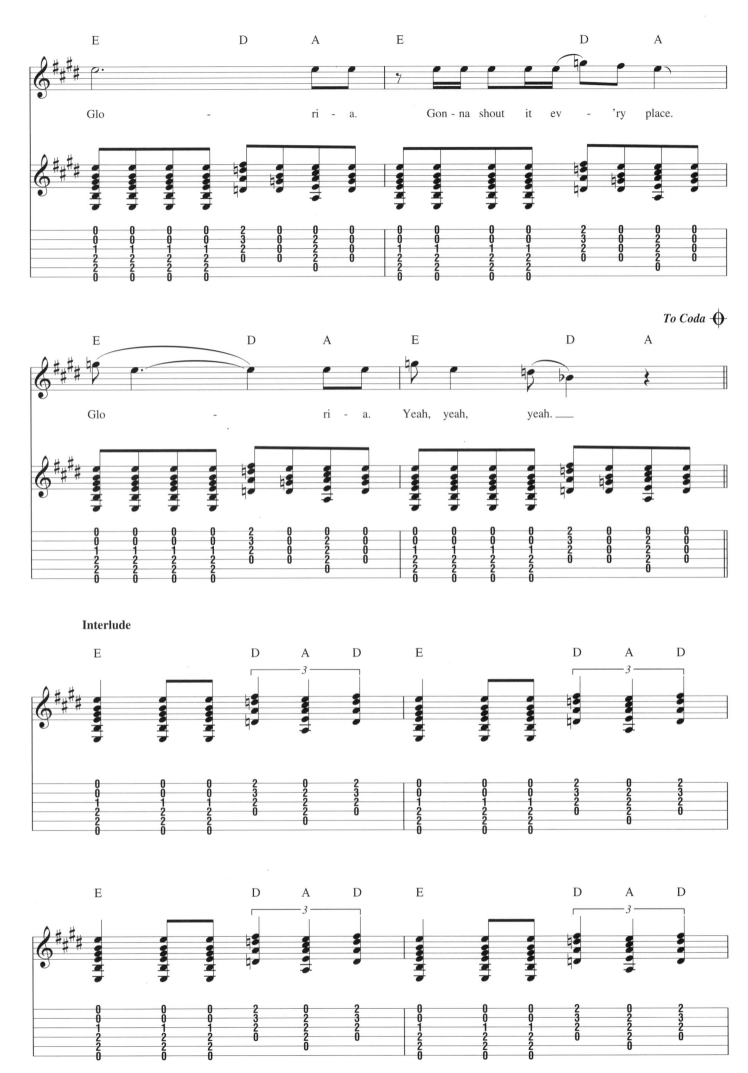

To Coda ⊕

Interlude

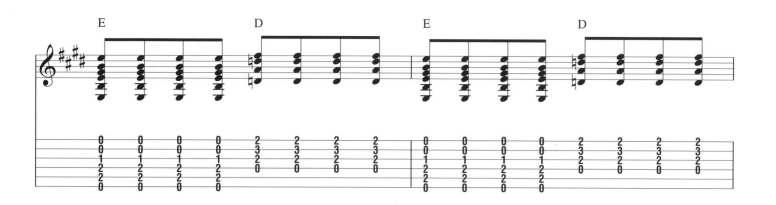

D.S. al Coda

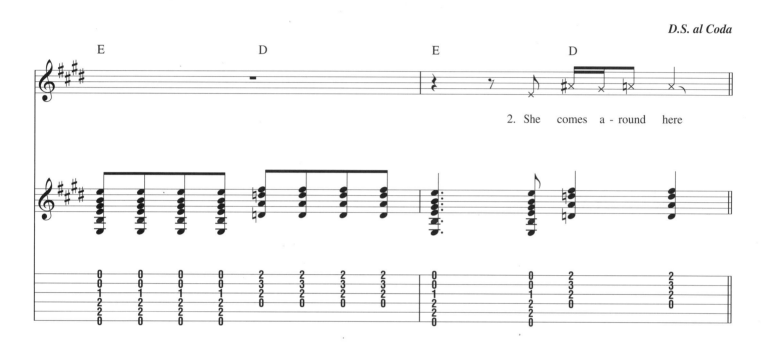

2. She comes a - round here

Coda

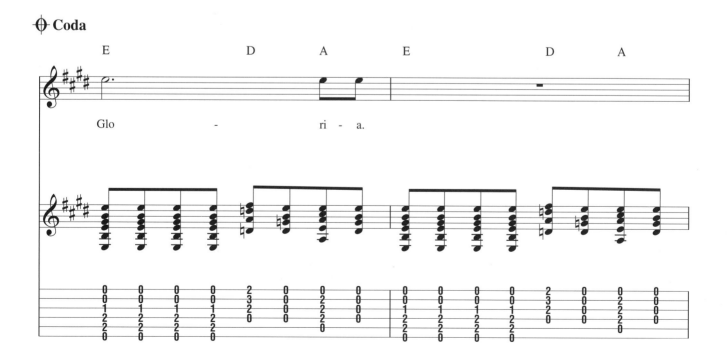

Glo - ri - a.

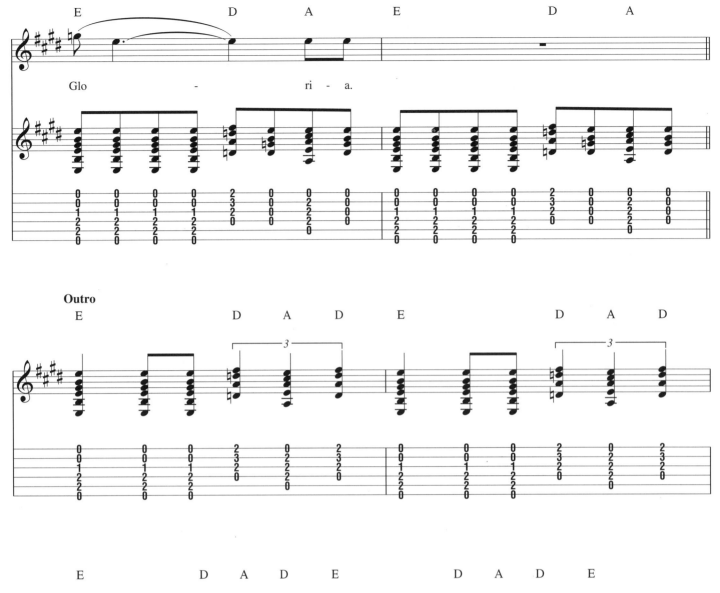

Outro

Additional Lyrics

2. She comes around here just about midnight.
   She make me feel so good.
   I wan' tell you she make me feel alright.
   Comes walkin' down my street.
   Why don' 'cha come up to my house?
   You knock upon my door.
   And then she call out my name,
   Then make me feel alright.
   G, L, O, R, I, A.

I Fought the Law

Words and Music by Sonny Curtis

Intro
Moderately fast ♩ = 147

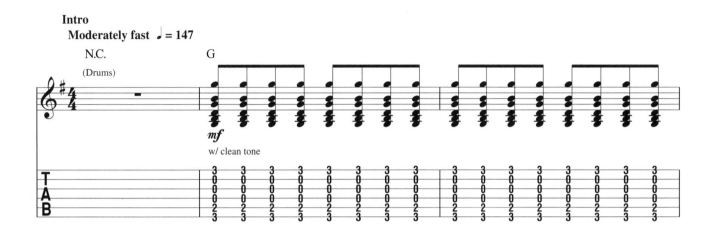

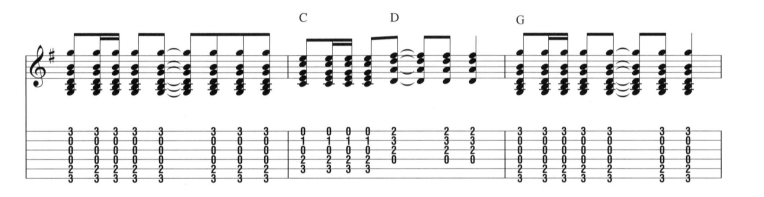

% Verse

2nd time, Gtr. tacet

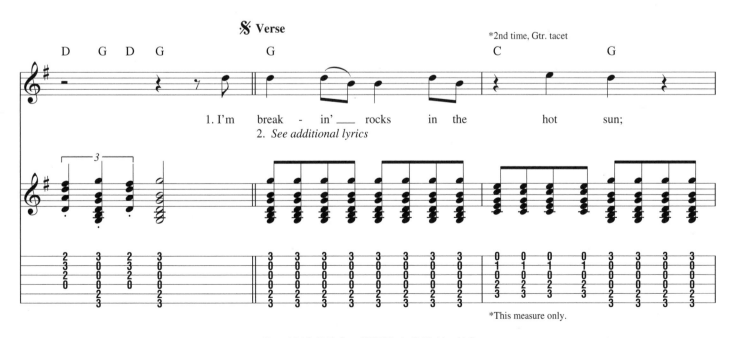

1. I'm break-in' ___ rocks in the hot sun;
2. *See additional lyrics*

*This measure only.

Copyright © 1961 Sony/ATV Music Publishing LLC
Copyright Renewed
All Rights Administered by Sony/ATV Music Publishing LLC, 8 Music Square West, Nashville, TN 37203
International Copyright Secured   All Rights Reserved

law won. I fought the law ___ and the law ___ won.

Bridge

I left my ba - by and I feel ___ so bad. ___ I

guess my race is run. ___ But she's the best ___ girl

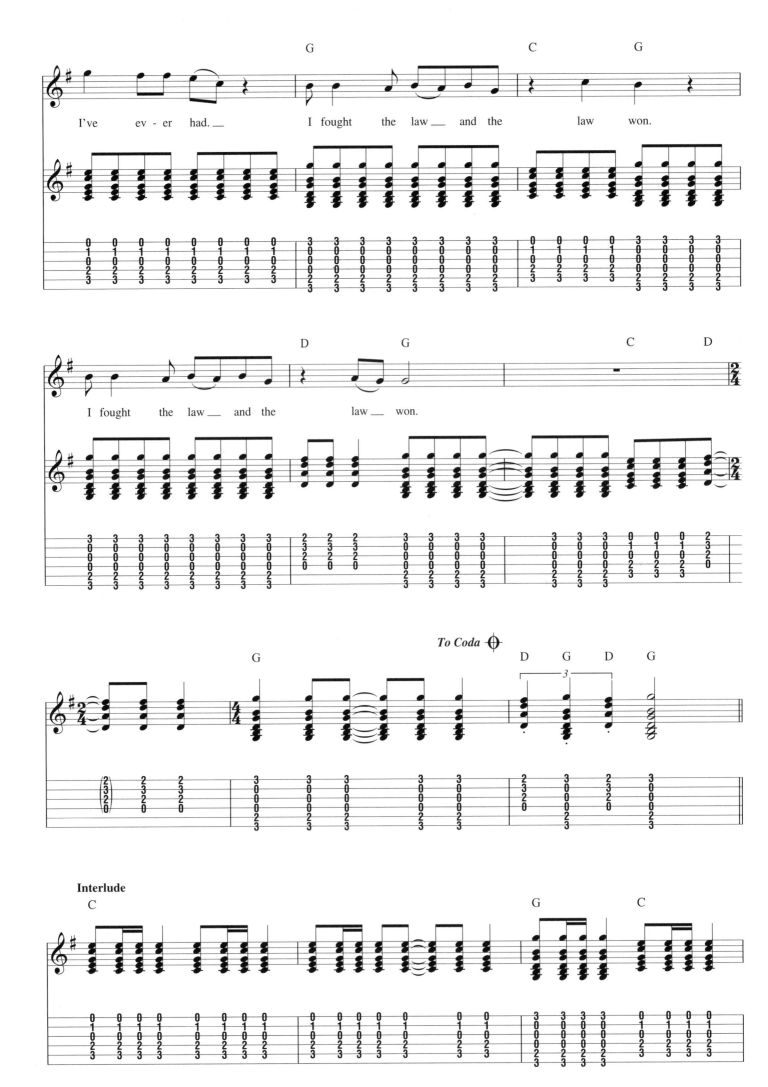

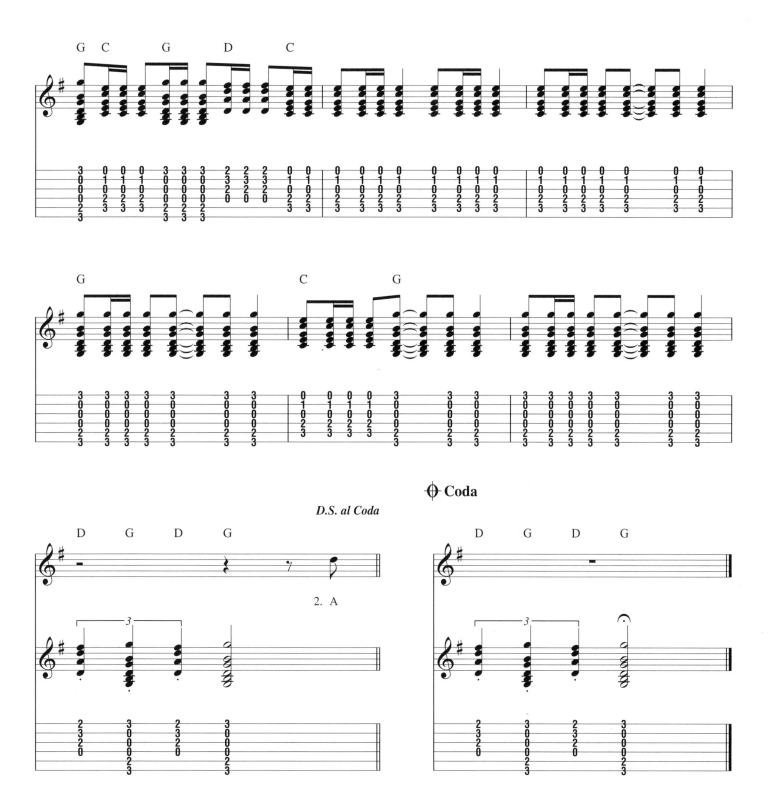

Coda

D.S. al Coda

Additional Lyrics

2. A robbin' people with a six-gun;
   I fought the law and the law won.
   I fought the law and the law won.
   I miss my baby and the good fun;
   I fought the law and the law won.
   I fought the law and the law won.

Love Me Do

Words and Music by John Lennon and Paul McCartney

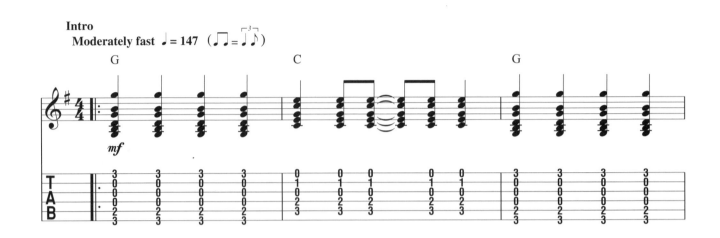

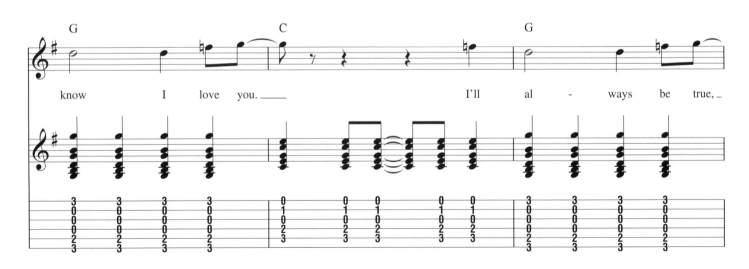

© 1962, 1963 MPL COMMUNICATIONS LTD.
© Renewed 1990, 1991 MPL COMMUNICATIONS LTD. and LENONO.MUSIC
All Rights for MPL COMMUNICATIONS LTD. in the U.S. and Canada Controlled and Administered by BEECHWOOD MUSIC CORP.
All Renewal Rights for LENONO.MUSIC in the U.S. Controlled and Administered by EMI BLACKWOOD MUSIC INC.
All Rights Reserved   International Copyright Secured   Used by Permission

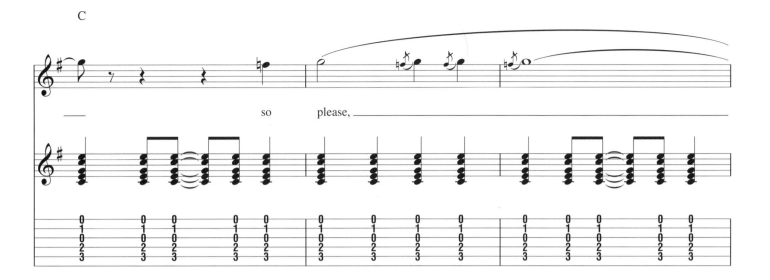

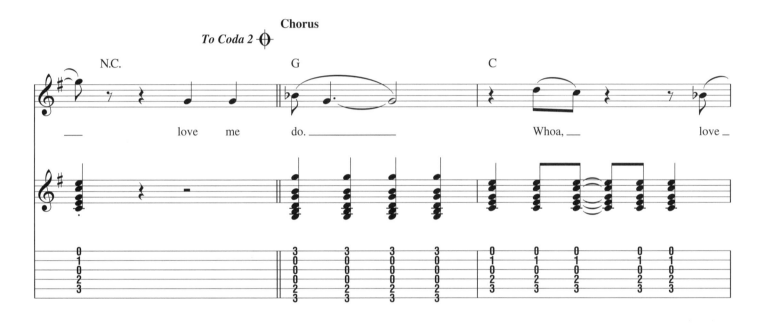

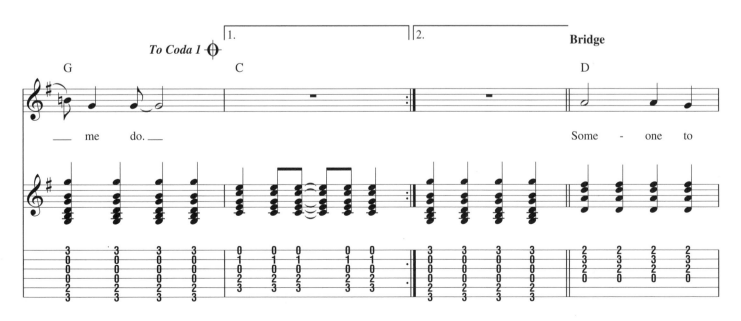

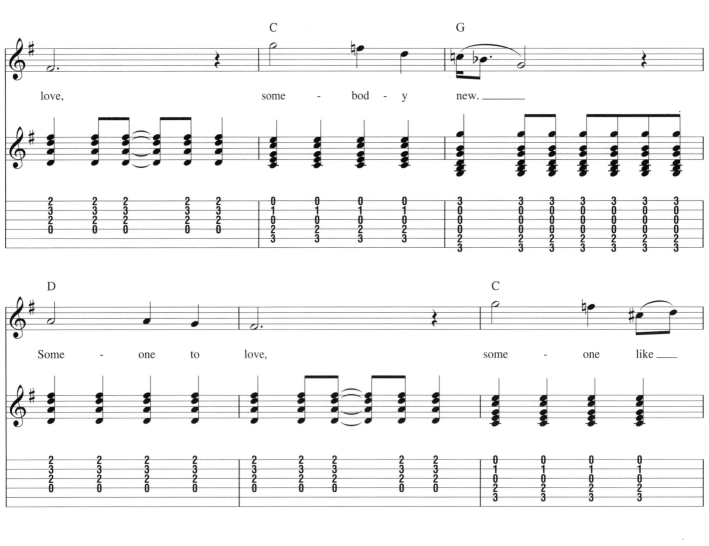

Coda 1

D.S. al Coda 1

Harmonica Solo

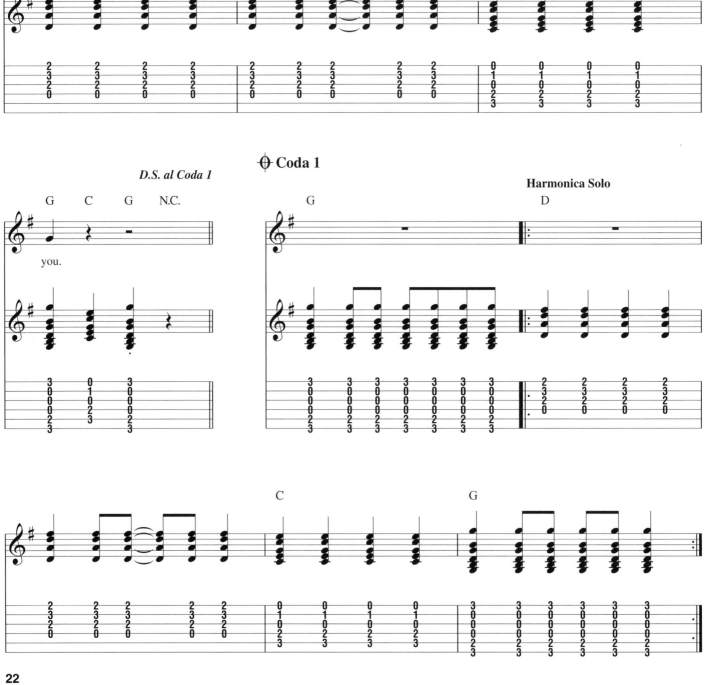

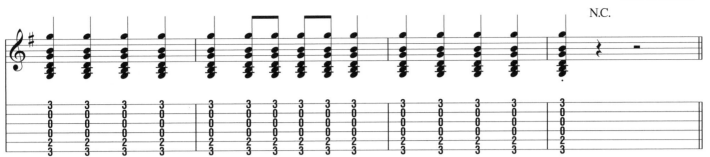

⊕ Coda 2

Chorus

do. _____ Whoa, _____ love _____ me do. _____

Yeah, _____ love me do. _____ Whoa. _____

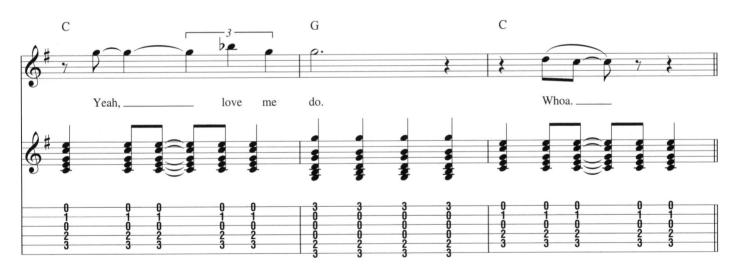

Outro

Repeat and fade

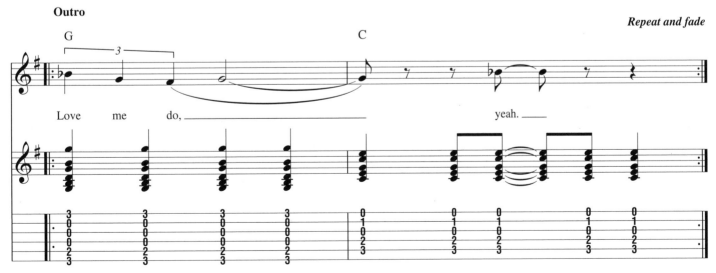

Love me do, _____ yeah. _____

Mellow Yellow

Words and Music by Donovan Leitch

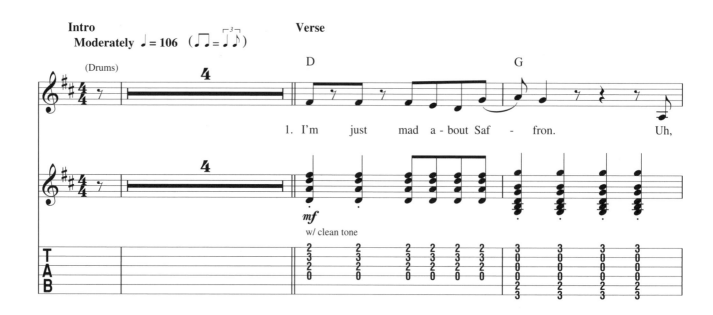

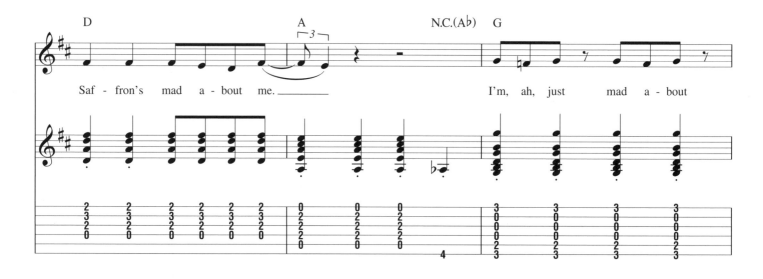

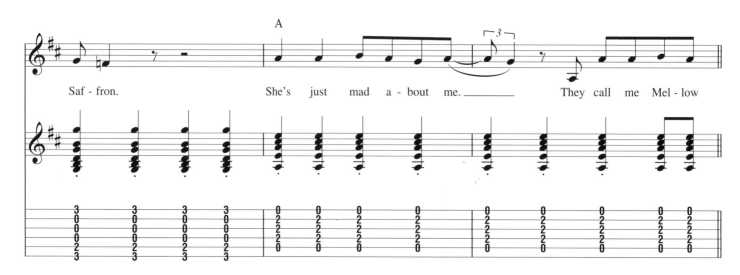

Copyright © 1966 by Donovan (Music) Ltd.
Copyright Renewed
All Rights Administered by Peer International Corporation
International Copyright Secured All Rights Reserved

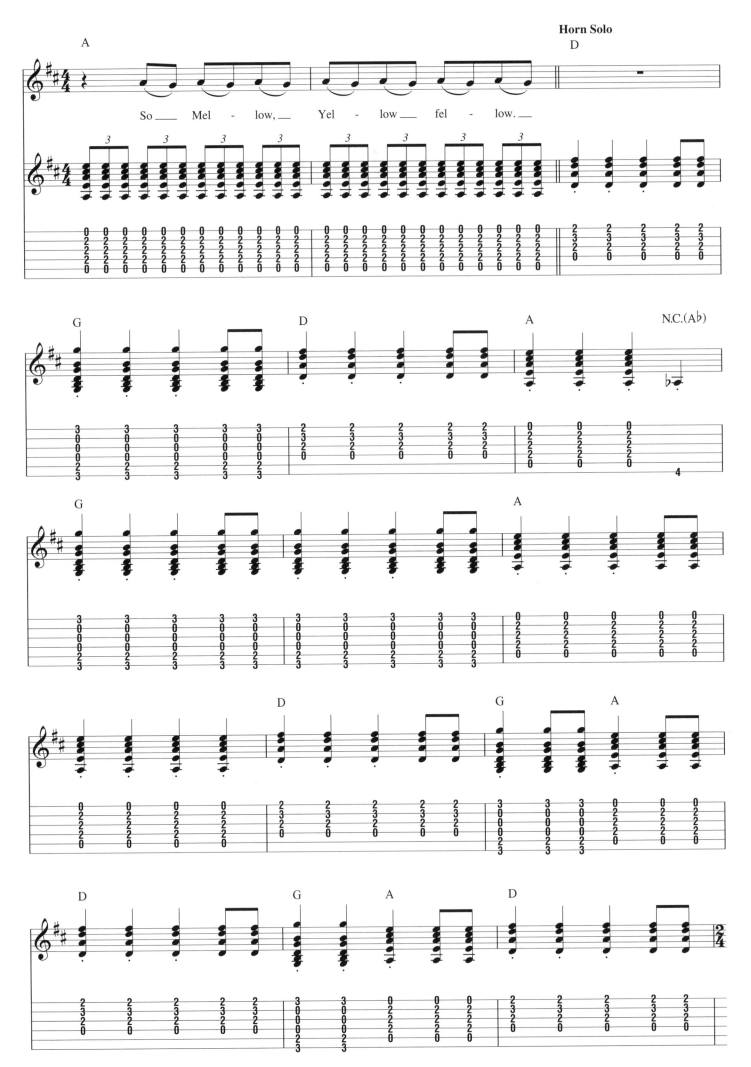

So __ Mel - low, __ Yel - low __ fel - low. __

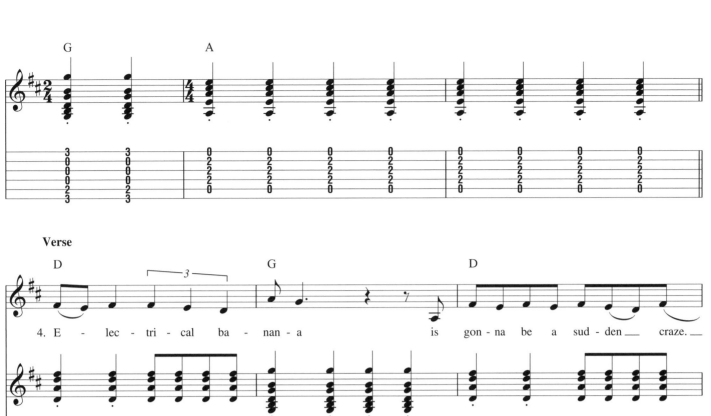

Verse

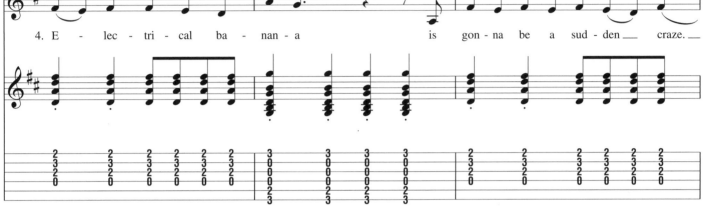

4. E - lec - tri - cal ba - nan - a is gon - na be a sud - den craze.

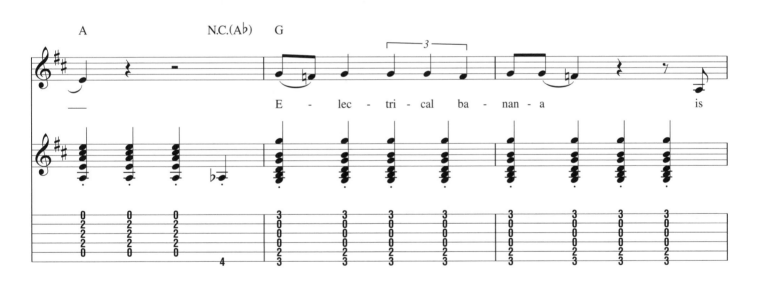

E - lec - tri - cal ba - nan - a is

Chorus

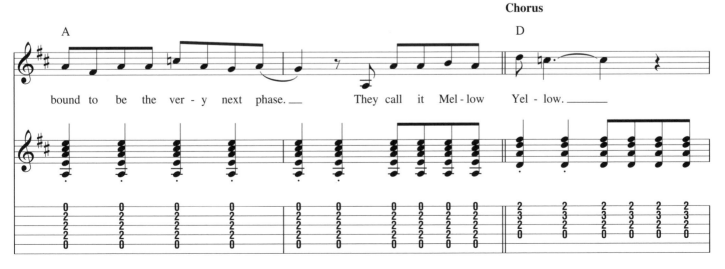

bound to be the ver - y next phase. They call it Mel - low Yel - low.

Stir It Up

Words and Music by Bob Marley

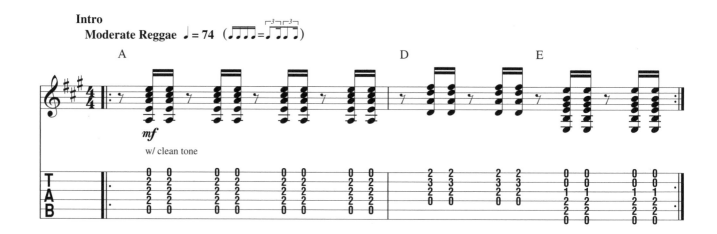

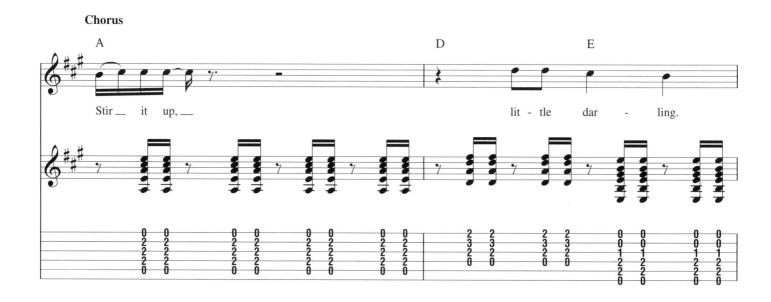

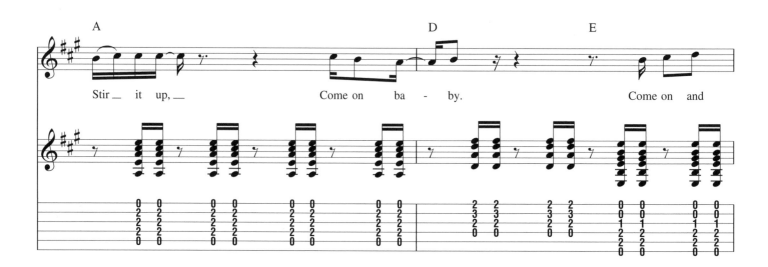

Copyright © 1972 Fifty-Six Hope Road Music, Ltd., Odnil Music, Ltd. and Blue Mountain Music, Ltd.
Copyright Renewed
All Rights in North America Administered by Fairwood Music USA (ASCAP) on behalf of Blue Mountain Music, Ltd. and throughout the rest of the world by
Fairwood Music Ltd. (PRS) on behalf of Blue Mountain Music, Ltd.
International Copyright Secured   All Rights Reserved

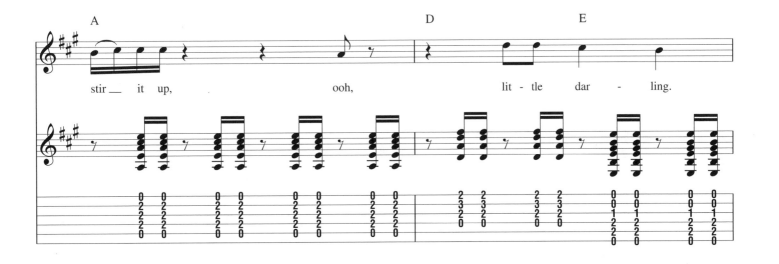

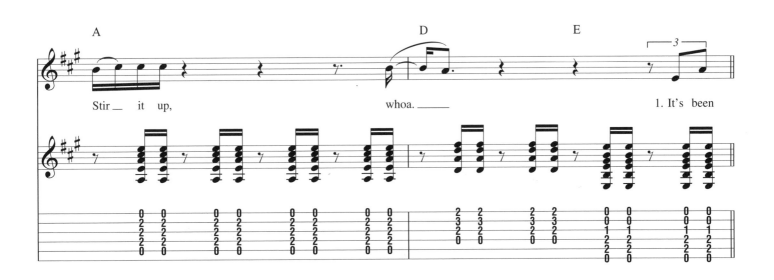

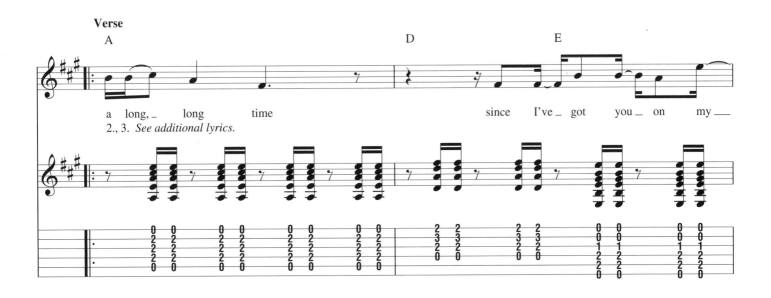

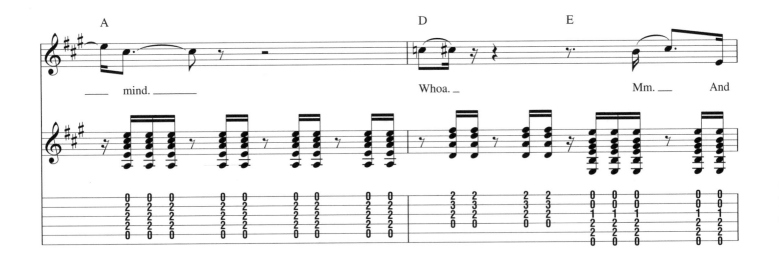

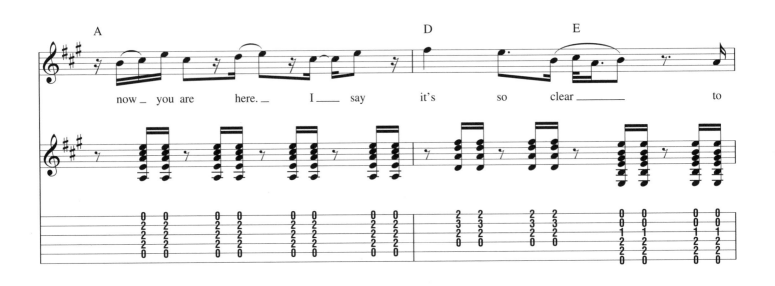

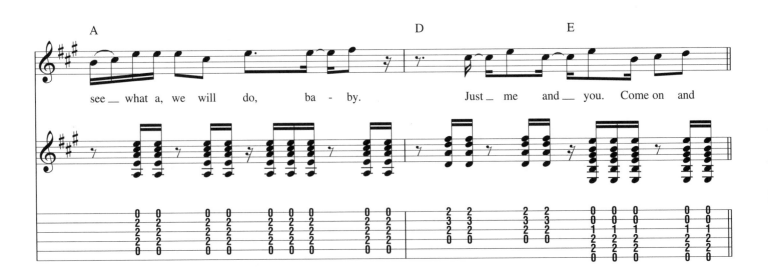

Chorus

stir __ it up,   I __ wan - na say,   lit - tle dar - ling, yeah.

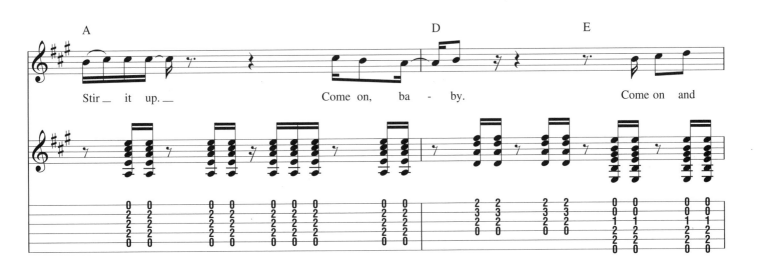

Stir __ it up. __   Come on,   ba - by.   Come on and

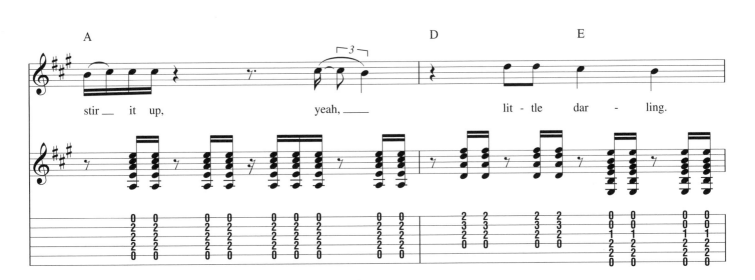

stir __ it up,   yeah, __   lit - tle dar - ling.

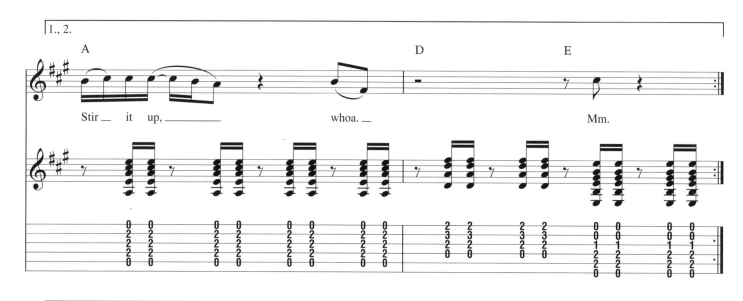

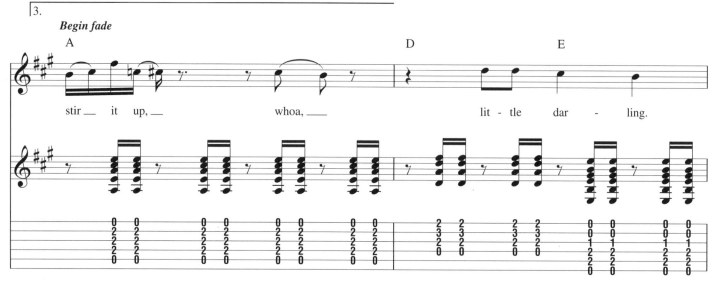

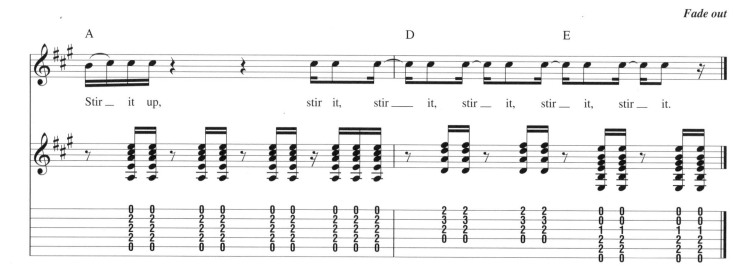

Additional Lyrics

2. I'll push the wood, and I'll blaze your fire.
   Then I satisfy your all desire.
   Said I stir it, yeah, ev'ry minute.
   All you've got to do, baby, is keep it in it and

Chorus 2. Stir it up. Come on, little darling.
   Stir it up. I'm already thirsty.
   Come on and stir it up, oh, oh. Little darling,
   Stir it up, whoa, mm.

3. And then quench me when I'm thirsty.
   Come on, cool me down, baby, when I'm hot.
   Your recipe, darling, is so tasty.
   And you sure can stir your pot.

Chorus 3. So, stir it up, oh, little darling.
   Stir it up. Come on, girl.
   Come on and stir it up, whoa, little darling.
   Stir it up, stir it, baby, stir it.
   Come on and...

You Don't Mess Around with Jim

Words and Music by Jim Croce

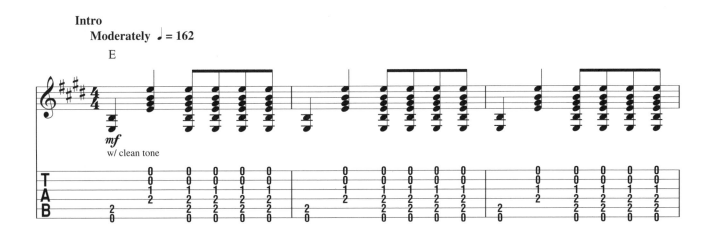

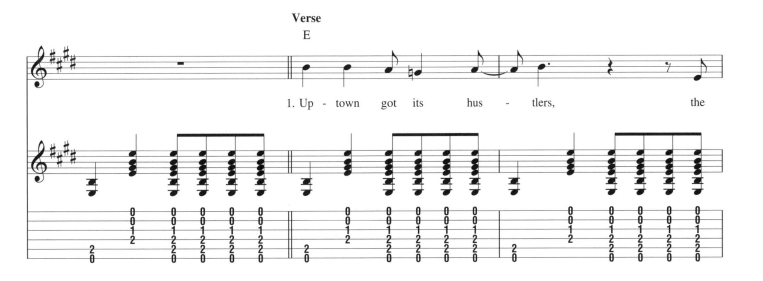

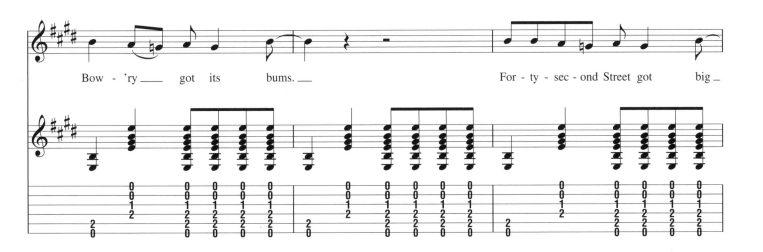

© 1971 (Renewed 1999) TIME IN A BOTTLE PUBLISHING and CROCE PUBLISHING
All Rights Controlled and Administered by EMI APRIL MUSIC INC.
All Rights Reserved   International Copyright Secured   Used by Permission

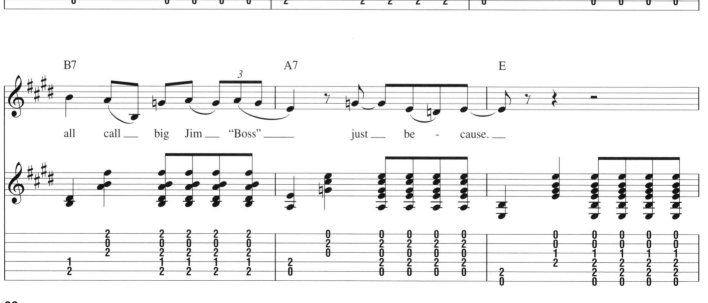

42

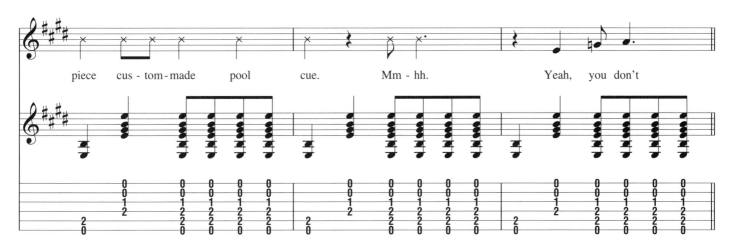

piece cus-tom-made pool cue. Mm-hh. Yeah, you don't

Coda

Outro

Mm, mm, mm, mm, — mm, mm, mm, mm. Mm, mm, mm, mm. —

Repeat and fade

Mm, mm, mm, mm, — mm, mm, mm, mm. Mm, mm, mm, mm. —

Additional Lyrics

3. Well, a hush fell over the poolroom,
   Jimmy come boppin' in off the street.
   And when the cuttin' were done,
   The only part that wasn't bloody was
   The soles of the big man's feet. Woo!
   Yeah, he were cut in 'bout a hundred places,
   And he were shot in a couple more.
   And you better believe they sung a diff'rent kind of story
   When a big Jim hit the floor.
   Oh. Now they say you don't...

Willie and the Hand Jive

Words and Music by Johnny Otis

© 1958 (Renewed 1986) ELDORADO MUSIC CO. (BMI)/Administered by BUG MUSIC
All Rights Reserved   Used by Permission

walk _ and stroll and Suz - ie Q, _____ 'n'

do __ that cra - zy Hand __ Jive, __ too. _____

𝄋 Verse

2. Ma - ma, ma - ma look at Un - cle Joe. He's a
3., 4. *See additional lyrics*

do - in' the Hand __ Jive with sis - ter Flo.

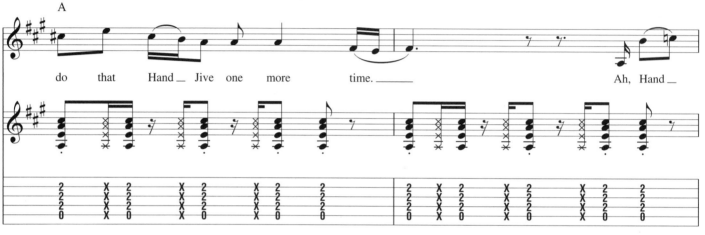

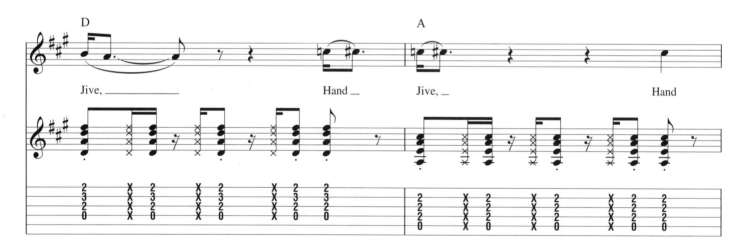

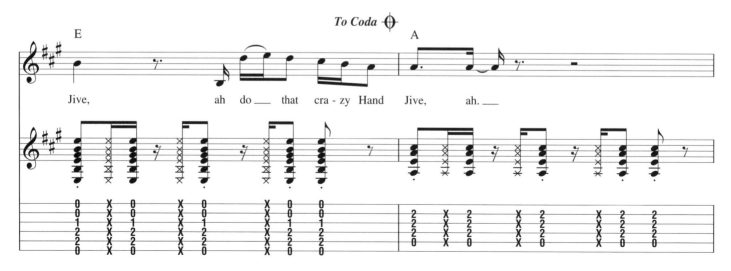

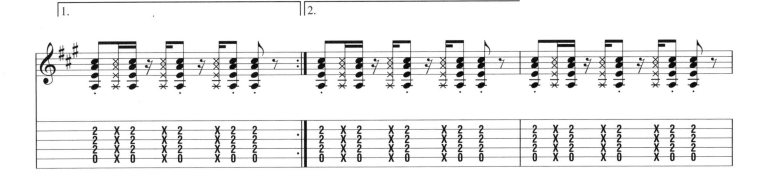

D.S. al Coda

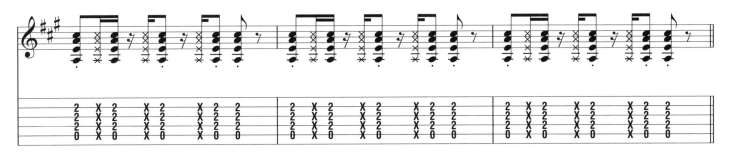

Coda

Outro-Guitar Solo

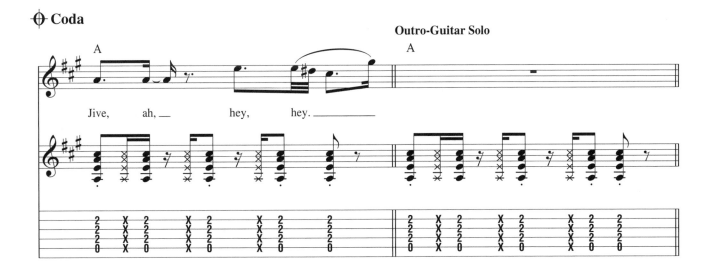

Jive, ah, — hey, hey. _____

Play 11 times

Repeat and fade

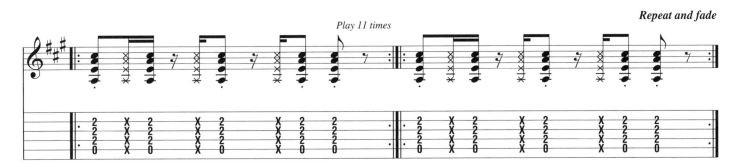

Additional Lyrics

3. Doctor and a lawyer and an injun chief,
   Ah, they all dig that crazy beat.
   Wayout Willie give 'em all a treat
   When he hit that Hand Jive with his feet.

4. Willie and Millie got married last fall.
   They had a Little Willie Junior and that ain't all.
   Well, the kids got crazy and it's plain to see,
   A doin' the Hand Jive on TV.

HAL•LEONARD GUITAR PLAY•ALONG

This series will help you play your favorite songs quickly and easily. **INCLUDES TAB** Just follow the tab and listen to the CD to hear how the guitar should sound, and then play along using the separate backing tracks. Mac or PC users can also slow down the tempo without changing pitch by using the CD in their computer. The melody and lyrics are included in the book so that you can sing or simply follow along.

VOL. 1 – ROCK	00699570 / $16.99	VOL. 45 – TV THEMES	00699718 / $14.95
VOL. 2 – ACOUSTIC	00699569 / $16.95	VOL. 46 – MAINSTREAM ROCK	00699722 / $16.95
VOL. 3 – HARD ROCK	00699573 / $16.95	VOL. 47 – HENDRIX SMASH HITS	00699723 / $17.95
VOL. 4 – POP/ROCK	00699571 / $16.99	VOL. 48 – AEROSMITH CLASSICS	00699724 / $14.95
VOL. 5 – MODERN ROCK	00699574 / $16.99	VOL. 49 – STEVIE RAY VAUGHAN	00699725 / $16.95
VOL. 6 – '90s ROCK	00699572 / $16.99	VOL. 50 – NÜ METAL	00699726 / $14.95
VOL. 7 – BLUES	00699575 / $16.95	VOL. 51 – ALTERNATIVE '90s	00699727 / $12.95
VOL. 8 – ROCK	00699585 / $14.95	VOL. 52 – FUNK	00699728 / $14.95
VOL. 9 – PUNK ROCK	00699576 / $14.95	VOL. 54 – HEAVY METAL	00699730 / $14.95
VOL. 10 – ACOUSTIC	00699586 / $16.95	VOL. 55 – POP METAL	00699731 / $14.95
VOL. 11 – EARLY ROCK	00699579 / $14.95	VOL. 56 – FOO FIGHTERS	00699749 / $14.95
VOL. 12 – POP/ROCK	00699587 / $14.95	VOL. 57 – SYSTEM OF A DOWN	00699751 / $14.95
VOL. 13 – FOLK ROCK	00699581 / $14.95	VOL. 58 – BLINK-182	00699772 / $14.95
VOL. 14 – BLUES ROCK	00699582 / $16.95	VOL. 59 – GODSMACK	00699773 / $14.95
VOL. 15 – R&B	00699583 / $14.95	VOL. 60 – 3 DOORS DOWN	00699774 / $14.95
VOL. 16 – JAZZ	00699584 / $15.95	VOL. 61 – SLIPKNOT	00699775 / $14.95
VOL. 17 – COUNTRY	00699588 / $15.95	VOL. 62 – CHRISTMAS CAROLS	00699798 / $12.95
VOL. 18 – ACOUSTIC ROCK	00699577 / $15.95	VOL. 63 – CREEDENCE CLEARWATER REVIVAL	00699802 / $16.99
VOL. 19 – SOUL	00699578 / $14.95	VOL. 64 – THE ULTIMATE OZZY OSBOURNE	00699803 / $16.99
VOL. 20 – ROCKABILLY	00699580 / $14.95	VOL. 65 – THE DOORS	00699806 / $16.99
VOL. 21 – YULETIDE	00699602 / $14.95	VOL. 66 – THE ROLLING STONES	00699807 / $16.95
VOL. 22 – CHRISTMAS	00699600 / $15.95	VOL. 67 – BLACK SABBATH	00699808 / $16.99
VOL. 23 – SURF	00699635 / $14.95	VOL. 68 – PINK FLOYD – DARK SIDE OF THE MOON	00699809 / $16.99
VOL. 24 – ERIC CLAPTON	00699649 / $16.95	VOL. 69 – ACOUSTIC FAVORITES	00699810 / $14.95
VOL. 25 – LENNON & McCARTNEY	00699642 / $14.95	VOL. 71 – CHRISTIAN ROCK	00699824 / $14.95
VOL. 26 – ELVIS PRESLEY	00699643 / $14.95	VOL. 72 – ACOUSTIC '90s	00699827 / $14.95
VOL. 27 – DAVID LEE ROTH	00699645 / $16.95	VOL. 74 – PAUL BALOCHE	00699831 / $14.95
VOL. 28 – GREG KOCH	00699646 / $14.95	VOL. 75 – TOM PETTY	00699882 / $16.99
VOL. 29 – BOB SEGER	00699647 / $14.95	VOL. 76 – COUNTRY HITS	00699884 / $14.95
VOL. 30 – KISS	00699644 / $14.95	VOL. 78 – NIRVANA	00700132 / $14.95
VOL. 31 – CHRISTMAS HITS	00699652 / $14.95	VOL. 80 – ACOUSTIC ANTHOLOGY	00700175 / $19.95
VOL. 32 – THE OFFSPRING	00699653 / $14.95	VOL. 81 – ROCK ANTHOLOGY	00700176 / $19.95
VOL. 33 – ACOUSTIC CLASSICS	00699656 / $16.95	VOL. 82 – EASY SONGS	00700177 / $12.95
VOL. 34 – CLASSIC ROCK	00699658 / $16.95	VOL. 83 – THREE CHORD SONGS	00700178 / $12.95
VOL. 35 – HAIR METAL	00699660 / $16.95	VOL. 96 – THIRD DAY	00700560 / $14.95
VOL. 36 – SOUTHERN ROCK	00699661 / $16.95	VOL. 97 – ROCK BAND	00700703 / $14.95
VOL. 37 – ACOUSTIC METAL	00699662 / $16.95	VOL. 98 – ROCK BAND	00700704 / $14.95
VOL. 38 – BLUES	00699663 / $16.95		
VOL. 39 – '80s METAL	00699664 / $16.95		
VOL. 40 – INCUBUS	00699668 / $16.95		
VOL. 41 – ERIC CLAPTON	00699669 / $16.95		
VOL. 42 – CHART HITS	00699670 / $16.95		
VOL. 43 – LYNYRD SKYNYRD	00699681 / $17.95		
VOL. 44 – JAZZ	00699689 / $14.95		

Prices, contents, and availability subject to change without notice.

FOR MORE INFORMATION, SEE YOUR LOCAL MUSIC DEALER, OR WRITE TO:

HAL•LEONARD® CORPORATION
7777 W. BLUEMOUND RD. P.O. BOX 13819 MILWAUKEE, WI 53213

Visit Hal Leonard online at www.halleonard.com

Complete song lists available online.

1208